A Home for Bonnie

Contents

F. R. Robinson • Photographs by Malcolm Cross

Lost

This is my dog, Bonnie. I got her from a Lost Dogs' Home.

Someone owned Bonnie before me, but
I don't know who it was. They did not
take very good care of her, and she
got lost.

Bonnie was found all alone. She was hungry and cold.

Waiting for a Home

Bonnie was taken to a Lost Dogs' Home. She was put in a cage and someone looked after her.

Bonnie was very quiet and she slept a lot of the time.

Her owners never came to get her.

I wanted a dog, so I went to the Lost Dogs' Home to look for one.

There was Bonnie!

Bonnie Comes Home

Now Bonnie had a home.

At first, she was very weak. She couldn't run and she didn't know how to play.

She was very quiet
and she slept almost
all the time.

I took very good care of Bonnie. I fed her well and made sure she had plenty of water to drink.

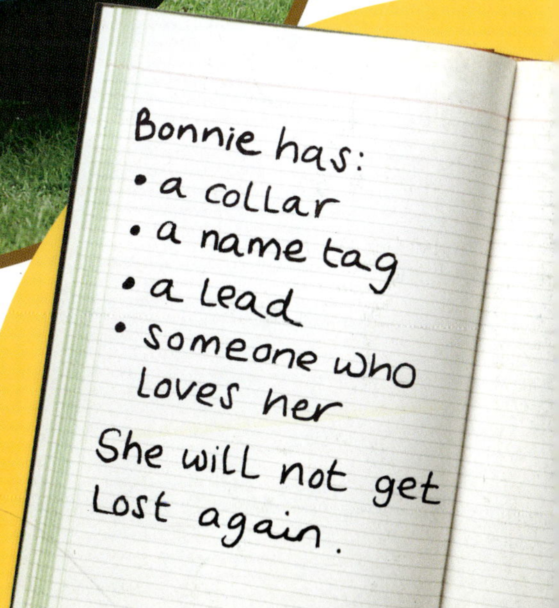

I took her for walks
in the park.

Bonnie has:
- a collar
- a name tag
- a lead
- someone who loves her

She will not get lost again.

Bonnie Now

I've had Bonnie for six months now.
She is much better.

She can run, but not very fast. She can
play, but just a little.

Now Bonnie is not so quiet. She barks when she wants something.

Bonnie still sleeps a lot. She's still getting better. The vet says that soon she'll be fine.

I love looking after Bonnie. She's a good friend to me.

Every dog needs these things to stay happy, safe and well:

a bed

a name tag

food

water

a collar

a lead

toys

someone to love them

Lost Pet

Information

What to do if you find a lost pet

- Never touch a lost animal. It might be sick, or it might try to bite you.
- Ask an adult to call the police or an animal rescue centre. They will take the animal to a safe place.
- Put up signs in shops and on lampposts. The signs should describe the lost animal, where you found it, and where it is now.

What to do if your pet is lost

- Check all the animal rescue centres in your area.
- Call the police. Ask them to look out for your pet.
- Put up signs in shops and on lampposts. The signs should have a picture of your pet and a phone number someone can call.

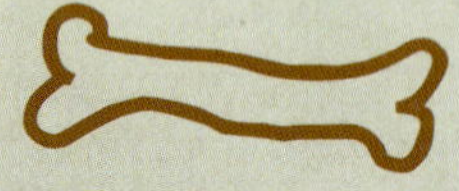